MW00526526

{ CITIESCAPE }

SINGAPORE*

{ CITIESCAPE }

MAT OAKLEY

CONTENTS*

VITAL
STATS*

NAME Singapore **AKA** The Lion City
DATE OF BIRTH Mid-13th century, when a minor
trading post was founded by the Srivijaya empire;
modern Singapore was established in 1819.
HEIGHT 10m **SIZE** 682 sq km
ADDRESS Singapore **POPULATION** 4.5 million

PEOPLE*

* A 'CHINESE' CITY IT MAY BE, BUT THE NUTS AND BOLTS OF SINGAPORE'S DEMOGRAPHICS – 77% Chinese, 14% Malay, 8% Indian – only tell half the story. It's a stew of seemingly mismatched ingredients, but among the babel of Mandarin, Tamil, Malay, Hokkien, Teochew, Cantonese and English, the forms of Mr and Mrs Typical Singaporean stand proud, pushing their way to the front, his mobile phone grafted onto his skull, her handbag stuffed with loyalty discount cards, while their Indonesian maid trails behind carrying the baby.

MODERN CAPITALISM FELL easily into the warm embrace of Singapore's Chinese and Indian cultures. The good old-fashioned graft that built the city has been handed over largely to immigrant labour – today's Singaporean, cynics will tell you, is a slave to the five Cs: career, car, condo, cash and credit card. To that, add one more C: chow.

9.

ANATOMY*

* EVIDENCE OF SINGAPORE'S FORMER IDENTITY, AS A SWAMP INFESTED WITH MOSQUITOES AND TIGERS, IS HARD TO FIND THESE DAYS.
The mangroves are mostly gone, though the centre of the island is filled with forests and reservoirs. Some of the hills have been shaved off and dumped into the sea, expanding the island by 120 sq km. Downtown Singapore remains much as Sir Stamford Raffles drew it, an orderly model of town planning without any grid-like dullness. Wide boulevards lined with extravagant colonial façades and shady parks intertwine with narrow lanes full of shophouses and five-foot-ways – delightful covered, archway-lined pavements designed to protect citizens from sun and rain.

SPLITTING THE CITY is the surprisingly large Singapore River, sedate and green, which empties into a choppy bay bobbing with pilot vessels, tugs and tourist junks. Buried underneath it all, the majestic MRT train system fans across the island, teaming up with the city's gleaming buses to form a transport system so cheap and efficient it would make a German blush.

PERSONALITY*

{ *CITIES OFTEN FALL VICTIM TO POPULAR WISDOM, WHICH CONDEMNS THEM TO BE KNOWN FOREVER BY A HANDFUL OF ADJECTIVES** with little basis in fact or experience. Singapore, people will tell you with an authoritative air, is 'sterile' and 'soulless' and above all, 'not The Real Asia'. (The Real Asia has poverty, dirt and an edge of danger to spice up travel tales back home.) And no conversation about the city is complete without the words 'chewing gum'. Everyone knows about the chewing gum ban, and the poor citizens whose lives have been cruelly bereft of its sticky freedoms. }

SINGAPORE IS HAPPY to surprise visitors, showing them what it's really like, dismantling the baggage of opinion people bring off the plane with them.

IT HAS THE best eating in Asia, a bustling arts scene, a rich architectural heritage, nightlife until dawn, peaceful island getaways, endless shopping, a thriving industry, nature reserves, a multicultural mix almost unparalleled in the region and, battering the

13.

final misconception into oblivion, a distinctly steamy side. Singapore is a city and a country all in one and, like one of those people who's mastered the art of packing, it has crammed an impossible amount into one small bag.

A SWAGGERING industrial and financial dynamo that has inspired admiration and envy across Asia and the rest of the world, Singapore's confidence has nevertheless been hard-earned. Racial tensions – inevitable when Malay, Indian, European and several different Chinese identities are thrown together and have to get along – have been trampled underfoot, however, by wealth, health and a level of personal security unknown elsewhere in Southeast Asia. And the rich cultural mix has inspired an obsession with food verging on the pathological: it's considered completely normal to drive from one side of the island to the other for a renowned chilli crab dish. Food is where the barriers are broken down and everyone speaks the same language.

STILL, THERE'S A force threatening Singapore far more hostile than any of its neighbours, and more merciless and fickle than any sabre-rattling foreign leader – it's called the global economy. For now, Singapore – chewing gum laws aside – is a jewel in the glittering crown of the free-market world. But the leaders of this thriving port city have had their eyes on their neighbours' history books, which chart the rise and rapid fall of the great trading centres of Melaka to the north and Jakarta to the south. They know how easily and how rapidly it could all end, and with the once-dominant manufacturing industry seeping away to emergent China, Vietnam and India, they know Singapore has to reinvent itself – and fast.

SINGAPORE HAS soft, callous-free hands and a wider streak of hedonism than it could ever afford before. It's slick, ultramodern and famously ultraclean – sample the city's persona for yourself in the chapters that follow.

MULTI CULTURAL *

{ *** EVER SINCE SIR STAMFORD RAFFLES LANDED NEAR THE MOUTH OF THE SINGAPORE RIVER IN 1819 AND HAD THE INSPIRED IDEA TO ESTABLISH THE** island as perhaps the modern world's first free-trade port, it has epitomised that worn old cliché, the melting pot. In the absence of a substantial indigenous population, there was no other way. }

TODAY, WATCHING GROUPS of Chinese, Straits Chinese, Malays, Indians and Europeans wander the streets and sit down to eat or share a beer, it's easy to forget that co-existence has not always come easily. In many ways it still doesn't, but there's nothing like economic success to paper over the cracks of ethnic division.

MORE THAN ANY other place, arguably, Singapore lives or dies by the success of its multiculturalism – fatal race riots in the 1960s inspired decades of government-imposed racial mixing that, to a large extent, have paid off.

17.

NOW, CHINESE, INDIAN AND MALAY Singaporeans do their National Service together, meet for Sunday afternoon football in the park, share tables at hawker centres and play in bands together. In a country whose demographics are dominated by the Chinese, the public voted a Malay boy the first Singapore Idol, ahead of his Chinese rival.

WHETHER IT'S despite or because of official policies, the Singaporean identity has emerged without destroying the traditions each group brought from its homeland. It finds itself on the sports field, in the waving crowds of the National Day parade, on the dinner table and, most distinctively of all, coming out of people's mouths.

THIS IS A CITY where people speak a version of English so different that even other English speakers can't understand a word of it – like the place itself, it's a soup of English, Hokkien, Mandarin, Malay and Tamil phrases. Cultural boundaries are equally fluid at mealtimes. Chinese friends flock to the roti prata stall for late-night flat bread and curry, and Malays and Indians suck down their fishball noodles with a serve of Hainanese chicken rice for lunch.

THIS IS NOT to say the city is colour-blind. If anything, its preoccupation with race and identity borders on obsession. But if you want to see the city's multicultural dream in action, to see men and women of different races sitting together with a common language and common purpose, just grab a seat in front of the big screen at a local pub on a Saturday night to watch a Liverpool game. They'll either be bouncing up and down in shared joy or united in their common misery.

18.

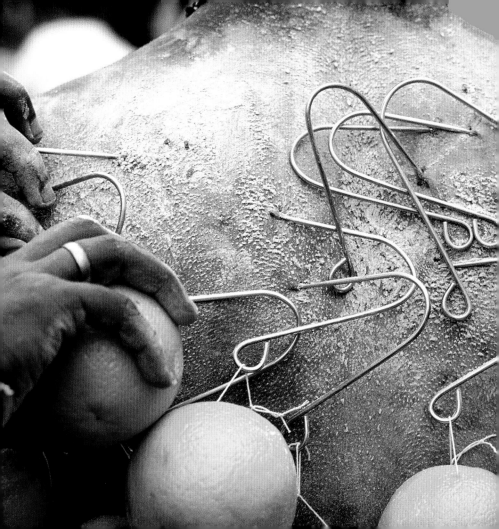

HAWKERS WELCOME*

{ *OF ALL SINGAPORE'S ADVANCES, ACHIEVEMENTS AND ACCOMPLISHMENTS, THE HAWKER CENTRE MAY GO DOWN AS ITS MOST DELIGHTFUL contribution to humanity. Once, hawkers were itinerant food-sellers, wandering the streets shouldering their ingredients, burners and a few stools and setting up wherever they were needed. They've long since gone, but it's bad news only for dedicated nostalgists, as modern hawkers have been corralled into teeming bazaars that offer possibly the best eating experience in Asia. }

THERE ARE FEW greater pleasures in life than sitting outside on a balmy evening, sipping your way through a succession of cool Tiger beers and tucking into a hawker centre meal. The array of Asian food on offer is so bewildering you could visit most hawker centres every day for a year and never have the same dish twice – whether you want Hokkien, Teochew or Hainanese, South Indian, Malay, Peranakan, vegetarian or grilled seafood. Don't expect fine china and a table to yourself, though: the centres are all about the food, nothing else.

21.

TO MARKET*

{ **✲ THE OVERPOWERING ODOURS OF THE CHINATOWN COMPLEX WET MARKET, OR THE SHEEP'S HEADS AND SLUICED GUTS** of the Tekka Market butcher stalls in Little India – what better antidote to the notion of 'sterile Singapore'? The old city dwells here: gruff 'uncles' hacking at meat, brusque 'aunties' at the vegetable stalls greeting customers with a 'What you wan' ah?' }

FLEA MARKETS DON'T have quite the same smell, but they do have the same jolly atmosphere, the crowds and the mix of customers. Sungel Road Thieves' Market is the most distinctive – a fascinating glimpse into Singapore's seedy side, with yet more grizzled 'uncles' trying to make the odd buck from an old record player or a shirt that nobody has worn for 50 years.

WITHOUT ANY SMELL at all, and carefully restored and polished to erase all signs of its ignoble past as a den of sin, Bugis Village Night Market is the place to pick up cheap clothes, CDs and watches, among a very orderly crowd of browsers.

22.

THE MIDDLE WAY*

{ *** WITH BUDDHISTS, TAOISTS, HINDUS, MUSLIMS AND CHRISTIANS ALL CRAMMED INTO A SMALL AREA,** in Singapore religious tolerance isn't so much a nice theory as an absolute necessity. Members of the different faiths rub shoulders and their houses of worship share postcodes – there's no room for hatred or segregation. Poisonous opinions, where they exist, are kept private, and those who voice them can be hauled into jail (as two bloggers found in 2005 when they published negative comments about the Malay community). Religious instruction is banned in schools and the state is officially Confucian, following a set of moral codes rather than a deity. }

ARCHITECTURALLY, Singapore's diversity has had wonderful effects: tiny Buddhist temples dot the housing estates, gleaming white churches grace the city centre and the Kampong Glam mosques stand proud with their striking domes. And of course, with so many different faiths, barely a month goes by without a holiday, festival or celebration.

GHETTO'N DOWN*

{ *IT BEGAN AS A DUBIOUS EXERCISE IN URBAN RACIAL ZONING, BUT IN THE }
MUDDLE OF RAMPANT EXPANSION AND DEVELOPMENT the firm demarcation
lines that Raffles drew on his town plan have had unexpectedly happy consequences.
Miniature countries have been preserved within the city, each a part of it, but each so
different it seems scarcely believable that they occupy the same metropolis.

VEGETABLES AND SPICES crowd the pavements of Little India, where fortune-tellers
promise riches and gold merchants aim to take them away. A few hundred metres
away, a waft of shisha smoke, the smell of thick, bubbling cardamom coffee and the
sudden rising note of a muezzin announces the Muslim quarter of Kampong Glam,
itself only a few blocks from the grand façades and the stately cricket oval of the British
colonial district. And in the streets of the public housing estates, the shuffling 'uncles'
in their stripy pyjama bottoms and white singlets sip coffee out of saucers and suck on
cigarettes.

FESTIVALS 'R' US*

{ }

*YOU CAN HARDLY STEP OUT THE DOOR IN SINGAPORE WITHOUT WALKING INTO A FESTIVAL, CELEBRATION OR CULTURAL EVENT. The pounding drums and lion dances of Chinese New Year, the dazzling floats of the Chingay street parade, the bizarre masochistic self-skewerings of the Hindu Thaipusam festival, the sheep-slaughtering ritual of the Muslim Hari Raya Haji holiday – and that's just in the first two months of the year. Add film, fashion, food, art and music festivals: every conceivable human cultural activity is boxed, wrapped and assigned two weeks on the calendar.

CYNICS JOKE that there is only one religious banner that unites the people of Singapore – the word 'SALE' in a shop window. A '70% off' sign inspires a devotion that knows no boundary of race or creed. There are plenty of opportunities to indulge that devotion, too – during the Great Singapore Sale, for example, merchants drop prices island-wide for eight whole weeks in June and July.

29.

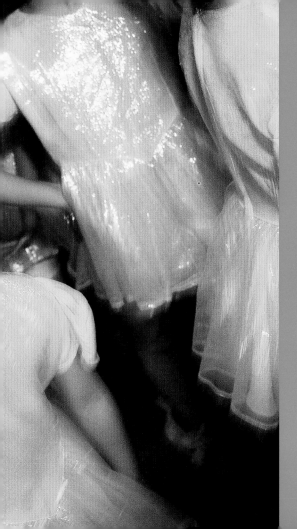

WHEN SINGAPORE SAYS street parade, it's going to be spectacular. And the biggest street parade of all is the Chingay Parade, or Parade of Dreams. On the 22nd day after Chinese New Year, Orchard Road rocks. Tiered temporary seating lines the road so that the thousands of onlookers can look down on the sumptuous floats and flag-bearers with their 12-metre-high flagpoles. There are stunningly beautiful dancers, bouncy lion acrobats, masked characters and cultural performers, youth art, fireworks, dragons and banners. Stunts are gravity-defying, moves are ground-breaking. It's all wild, exotic and absolutely glorious.

RAFFLES*

{ *** RAFFLES HOTEL'S SPOTLESS WHITE FACADE, WITH ITS IMMACULATE SIKH DOORMAN,** invites little gasps of surprise when you first catch sight of it amid the modern cityscape. It's a little pocket of preserved history, conjuring a lost world of adventurers, foreign royalty, tigers lurking beneath bars, high-society scandal and grand political schemes hatched over cigars and brandies. }

THE ILLUSION is spoiled somewhat these days by fat couples in leisurewear and tennis shoes, but the spirit of the days of Somerset Maugham and Joseph Conrad lives on. This Arab trader's bungalow, transformed into a hotel by four Armenian brothers, has become the ultimate image of the city. Even though it's a bit of a cliché, a visit to Singapore isn't complete without a sickly pink Singapore Sling in the Long Bar.

THE SHOPHOUSE *

{ *** THEY WERE ALMOST LOST TO THE 1970s LOVE AFFAIR WITH URBAN CONCRETE BOXES,** but the city realised just in time that shophouses look nice and make a handy modern tourism marketing tool. These multicoloured Chinese, Peranakan and Malay structures, with their crumbling walls, shuttered windows, canopied walkways and elaborate friezes, are the definitive 'old Singapore' building. }

THEY WERE ORIGINALLY designed with a shop or business on the lower floor and accommodation upstairs, and often had a canopy projecting over the footpath to shield pedestrians from the sun and rain. Many now function as offices for architects, design houses and boutiques, but most have kept their original flavour, with only a few licks of paint and some modern sanitation to set them apart from their forebears.

HDB ESTATES *

{ *** THE HDB (HOUSING AND DEVELOPMENT BOARD) ESTATE IS THE PETRI DISH OF SINGAPORE'S SOCIAL EXPERIMENT.** Clean, orderly, safe, well maintained and rigorously multiracial, these high-rise miniature towns break the mould. Even the vending machines work. With bustling shopping strips, food courts and community centres, this is the Singapore most Singaporeans know, part of the unspoken deal the population has made with its government. }

MORE THAN ONE MILLION units have been built in HDB estates for the citizens and sold to them at subsidised rates, giving the island one of the highest rates of home-ownership in the world. Some of them are concrete boxes with rudimentary furniture, housing large extended families; others have been transformed by their yuppie couple owners into trendy pads. All of them, for 84% of the population, are home.

SLICK*

{ *THERE'S VIRTUALLY NO SUCH THING AS A FARMER IN SINGAPORE. Though the city bursts with greenery and large pockets of undisturbed nature, the vast majority of Singaporeans are a strictly urban and often pampered breed, desperately attached to the comforts and conveniences of their modern metropolis. They like their cars, their gadgets and their cable TV, their movies and most of all, their shops. }

TELL A SINGAPOREAN that you're going to Laos, for instance, and they'll likely screw up their face and say, 'Why lah? No shopping there.' Show a Singaporean a little grass snake or a spider and they may well run screaming to the safety of the Lexus.

IT WASN'T ALWAYS this way. A generation or two ago, deadly snakes, virulent tropical diseases, poor sanitation and man-eating tigers were part of life on this steamy island, along with rampant vice and Chinese gang warfare. There again, even today country-club golfers might find themselves sharing the fairway with a king cobra. On rare cool days,

39.

{ truckers find pythons wrapped blithely around their engines for warmth. Urban jungle it may be, but in Singapore the jungle is sometimes closer than you think. }

MANY CRITICS OF Singapore have said that because it's basically an Asian city, it could only succeed by peopling itself with automatons who would rely on a nannying and bullying government to do their thinking for them. While it's true that Singaporeans have handed over a certain level of freedom to the government, this hardly impinges on the average person's lifestyle. They eat, they drink, they go wherever they like – as long as it's not too dangerous! Singaporeans can go out dancing till 4am, drink until dawn – even the world's oldest profession is legal.

THE FAMOUSLY URBAN, well-off lifestyle of Singaporeans is an object lesson in the transformative power of big government. While it does have its downside, it has also brought health, education, the world's second-busiest port, high finance, a thriving arts scene and fancy late-night nightclubs, healthy pensions, government payouts and a level of protection not afforded to other citizens of Southeast Asia.

THE MESSAGE IS out there: Singapore has arrived. But its success is always tempered by the shadow of uncertainty. Unlike large countries, Singapore can't afford a slump – it has no other cities to take up the slack. The neighbours also cause a persistent nervous tic. To the north is the fractious mass of Malaysia, with which Singapore has a history of squabbles, diplomatic brinkmanship and downright enmity; on all other sides is Indonesia, with its vast forces and fluctuating stability. In physical terms, Singapore is an ant – albeit a heavily armoured one – coexisting with elephants.

MOVIE MANIA*

{ ***BOLLYWOOD EXTRAVAGANZAS. HOLLYWOOD BLOCKBUSTERS. CHINESE, HONG KONG, JAPANESE AND KOREAN CROWD PLEASERS,** arthouse hits from around the world and adult films. Singaporeans go to the movies more often than anyone else in the world – eight times a year, on average, or about 36 million movie tickets. Movies are so popular they've even started showing them at two in the morning. It's surprising really, given that the average cinema experience is an endurance test involving subzero temperatures, glowing mobile phone screens, whispered audience commentaries, deleted sex scenes and ad sessions almost as long as the movie itself. }

EACH APRIL the Singapore International Film Festival brings an enormous collection of independent films to the city; outdoor mini-festivals are also held at times in Fort Canning Park. To help the local film industry get a slice of the action, the government established the Singapore Film Commission in 1998 – already Eric Khoo's films, for example, such as 2005's *Be With Me*, have had some success in Cannes.

天羅
飛沙劍陽紅

演王江君　　家達
龍兒剛俠龍烈

星期日加映早坊辜十

銀潤色彩
中巫片
上英文

THE INVISIBLE FEMINIST

IN COLORSCOPE WITH
MALAY ENGLISH CHINESE SUBTITLES

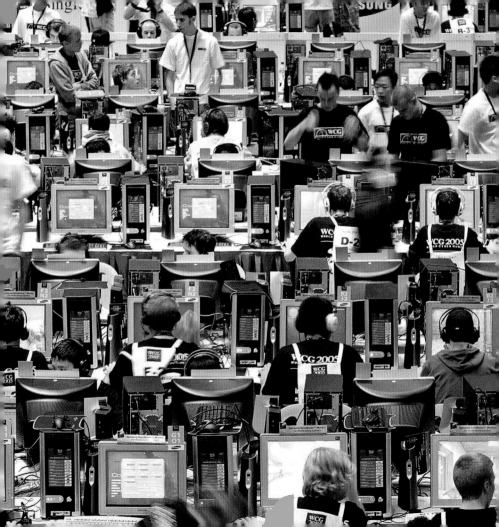

GO GO GADGETS*

{ ***ON THE TRAIN, IN A CAR, WALKING ALONG A STREET, BROWSING THROUGH A SHOP, WAITING AT A BUS STOP:** in almost every setting, faces are glued to small screens, wires stick out of heads and fingers play with buttons. If they ever invent virtual reality helmets that can replace the real world, we know who'll buy them first. }

THERE'S A CONCERN in the city that Singapore's youth have not developed their own popular culture, but are influenced instead, for example, by animation and manga from Japan, reality shows from America, Australia's surf and beach lifestyle, Malaysia's music. Well, one thing's clear: youth culture has mobile phones seriously embedded in it and marketers are scrambling to further alter their best customers' communication patterns. If they get their way, the latest phones will not only make video calls, play TV and send video clips, but also have GPS and function as a smart card or a security device. It's virtual reality without the helmet, ensuring last month's new mobile model is next month's second-hand discount special.

45.

MONEY MONEY MONEY*

{ * **WHO SAID SIZE MATTERS? FOR A COUNTRY LESS THAN HALF THE SIZE OF GREATER LONDON,** Singapore generates and handles staggering amounts of money, and has a per capita GDP greater than New Zealand or Spain and almost equal to that of the UK and Australia. Raffles Place, a former swamp that was drained, flattened, filled in and planted in 1824, used to be the home of the city's horse auctioneers. Now the money men take their breathers there, swilling quick coffees and sandwiches outside the dizzying glass towers before hurrying back into the air-conditioning. }

ITS REPUTATION for low corruption, a stable currency, low inflation and low interest rates has helped Singapore become a key Asian financial centre. Add to that its success as a major port, its huge investment in petroleum-refining and shipbuilding, and its development as a major manufacturing centre, and you get a nation with one of the highest standards of living and homeownership levels in the world.

QUAYS
TO THE CITY *

{ *** IMAGES OF THE RIVER AS A TRADING CENTRE ARE TODAY CONSIGNED TO SEPIA PHOTOGRAPHS IN FASHIONABLE GALLERIES.** Up until the 1960s, the quays were packed with jet-black bumboats ferrying rice, tea, tobacco or coffee to godowns (warehouses), so numerous they obscured the water altogether. The only cargo they now carry is tourists; the businesses have shifted to hi-tech cargo centres elsewhere on the island. }

THE TRADERS STILL fill the quays at midday and sundown, but now they wear striped shirts and expensive watches and deal in things they never hold in their hands. The river is no longer black and stinking. Chefs are in charge, not chiefs, and the main commodity at Boat, Clarke and Robertson is raucous good times: the only raw materials involved are food and drink. They're places to spend money rather than make it.

49.

ALL NIGHT LONG*

{ ***TO QUOTE ONE GOVERNMENT MINISTER'S INFAMOUS COMMENT, SINGAPORE HAS A 'SERIOUS FUN BUSINESS'.** Ultracool megaclubs such as Ministry of Sound, Attica and Zouk attract lines of the rich and the beautiful. There are miniskirts and midriff tops and men with square-toed shoes, large wallets and hopeful expressions. Inside, it's drunken, it's loud, it's raunchy and thoroughly 'un-Singaporean' – they even allow women to dance on bartops. }

MAYBE YOU'LL drink and dance until dawn in the city's pubs and clubs. Perhaps you'll quietly sip a cocktail on the veranda of the Bar and Billiard Room at Raffles, and ponder walking around the corner and up 70 floors for a cigar, vintage port and some of the best city views in Southeast Asia at the City Space Bar. While you're out, spare a thought for fellow revellers in Bangkok, who are turfed onto the streets at midnight.

51.

FANTASY ISLAND*

{ *** IT USED TO BE KNOWN IN MALAY AS THE 'THE ISLAND BEHIND WHICH LIES DEATH',** because of the malaria epidemics that almost wiped out the villagers who lived there. Now called Sentosa (management probably suspected The Island Behind Which Lies Death would be difficult to market), it's now a tourist icon of man-made beaches and theme attractions. }

LIKE ITS BEACHES of imported sand, Sentosa is an almost entirely synthetic attraction, but it still draws locals and tourists. They love the aquarium, where you can hop in with the sharks and dugongs if you dare. They play on the main golf courses and fun mini-courses, ride the free transport around the island and kick back to watch the nightly musical fountain with its spectacular sound, light and laser show. Sentosa has a tropical ambience and a butterfly park, but beware the nature walks – long-tailed macaque monkeys will stalk you for your food.

SINGAPORE
SIRENS*

{ * **IT'S ONE OF THOSE FACTS THAT CONFOUND POPULAR BELIEF, THAT CAUSE VISITORS TO KNOT BROWS IN CONFUSION.** Prostitution is legal in Singapore. However, it's a very Singaporean prostitution, with five demarcated red-light districts, 200 licensed brothels and around 6000 licensed prostitutes who carry health cards tracking their compulsory check-ups. And like domestic maids – another job nobody wants – prostitutes must be imported from Indonesia, Thailand and the Philippines. }

SINGAPORE'S STAID IMAGE, once entirely justified, is out of date. All-night beach parties draw people from Bangkok, while locals and visitors flock to European dance clubs and nude shows like the Crazy Horse Cabaret from France. Since the licensing laws were relaxed, some say the city has overtaken Bangkok as Southeast Asia's night-life capital, with long happy hours and clubs that stay open through to breakfast. Outdoor rave parties, usually held on Sentosa, are another big drawcard; city clubs are often modelled on the hippest New York clubs.

54.

THANKS TO THE Singapore government's tight control over development zoning, there are numerous areas given over almost entirely to bars, clubs and restaurants. On a pub crawl you won't have to walk more than 300 metres all night, and the area will be heaving with people. The quays are popular (Clarke Quay offers patrons giant lily pads to sit on while they sip their cocktails), or you can join the club crowd to party on a beach. It will be an artificial one, but the club crowd doesn't care.

ULTRA MODERN*

{ *ALWAYS GOING PLACES, ALWAYS ON THE LOOKOUT FOR THE NEXT NEW THING, BUT ALWAYS WITH ONE EYE ON HISTORY,** Singapore treads into the future with a curious mixture of urgency and caution – knowing it has no choice but to move forward, but prodding the ground anxiously before it does. }

WHILE SOCIAL PROGRESS may be slow, one thing Singapore is not afraid of is technology. Almost every bureaucratic function – applying for a marriage licence, registering a new company, booking a football pitch, filing your tax return – is done online. Down at the port, computers control and track every movement of every container, and their contents are monitored by hi-tech scanners. Even the bus fare system is controlled via satellite.

SINGAPOREANS SEEM TO be perpetually attached to gadgets, and it's not for nothing that the city is known throughout the world as a mecca for electronics bargain-hunters. And even though the mercury never dips below 25°C, the city's winter fashions are always up to date.

59.

NO-ONE COULD accuse Singapore of misty-eyed nostalgia, but its future is constantly informed by its past. Whenever outsiders are confused by an attitude, a policy, or a reaction, the explanation can often be found in the pages of history. The present-day order and success is tempered by a vivid collective memory of hardship, vulnerability, war, occupation and struggle, inspiring a determination to preserve its achievements.

ITS SLICK, MODERN lifestyle lies on a bedrock of shrewdness and hard graft that has shaped the unsentimental, go-getting attitudes of its citizens today. Hop a few branches up the family tree of most Singaporeans and you'll find people who came from other countries to make their mark, however small, in a steamy, tropical free-trading port riddled with vice, drugs and gang wars, their labours overseen by men in pith helmets and khaki.

WAR, JAPANESE OCCUPATION, liberation and the traumas of independence are still fresh in the minds of many mothers, fathers and grandparents. Like older generations everywhere, they bemoan the complacency and softness of their offspring, who have no idea what it was like.

DESTINATION: AIRPORT *

{ * **SINGAPORE? NEVER BEEN THERE, BUT THE AIRPORT WAS FANTASTIC. AIRPORTS AROUND THE WORLD ARE NOW TURNING THEMSELVES** into 'experiences' rather than places where you stand in queues and board planes, and it was Changi that started it all. Showers, hotel-lobby-like comfort, swimming pools and Jacuzzis, free city tours, nap rooms, free Internet, mini-cinemas – a lot of the things modern airports take for granted and lesser airports aspire to first appeared here. }

IT'S NOT JUST FACILITIES. Baggage arrives in minutes, the immigration queues are invariably short and quick, and, to the surprise of many, there is no noticeable customs counter. Changi is now anxiously looking over its shoulder at its rivals – Dubai, Qatar, KL, Bangkok's massive new (and trickily named) Suvarnabhumi Airport – all of which are eager to knock it off its perch. They have a way to go yet.

SHIPPING MAGNET *

{ *** FOUR HUNDRED SHIPS A DAY, A THIRD OF THE WORLD'S OIL, 200 SHIPPING LINES WITH LINKS TO 123 COUNTRIES,** about 1000 ships in port at any one time – this is Singapore's port, a cornerstone of the economy for nearly 200 years. Huge vessels crowd and surround the island like an invasion fleet, waiting for their turn to dock at this gateway to Asia. }

SINGAPORE'S STRATEGIC LOCATION was the reason the city was founded by the British in the first place. Since then, its efficient services and cargo-handling, stable government, pro-business environment and state-of-the-art telecommunications have combined to make it a centre for global shipping activities.

OLD BUMBOATS STILL belch along like echoes of the past though, reminding the city where it all started as they ferry tourists up and down the Singapore River or out to the surrounding islands.

ESPLANADE THEATRE*

{ *TWO MISSHAPEN DOMES, GLOWING GREEN IN THE DARK AND COVERED IN MENACING SPIKES,** announced to the world in 2003 that Singapore was a capital of culture, not merely commerce. The Esplanade theatre is a quirky retort to the staid colonial piles and square glass columns of finance surrounding it. }

THOUGH THE BUILDING is nicknamed, rather aptly, 'the Durians' after the pungent spiky fruit, the roofline of the $600-million arts complex was intended to mimic 'the way feathers on a bird's neck gradually change', according to the project's director.

THE CONTROVERSIAL exterior is made from 7139 angled aluminium shades that maximise the natural light while shielding the glass roof. The interior has that awe-inspiring atmosphere you get in a truly special building. The twin auditoriums are visually and acoustically spectacular – they rest on rubber pads to soak up external noise and vibration. All up, the complex is a shining example of the artsy, creative side of the city.

67.

COLONIAL
COUNTERPOINT *

{ * **THERE ARE MANY MOMENTS OF CONTRAST IN SINGAPORE, WHERE TIME SUDDENLY BECOMES SOMETHING VISIBLE AND CONCRETE,** where what was provides a clearer perspective on what is. Looking across the mouth of the bay from the Esplanade theatre to the majestic old Fullerton Hotel. Watching a giant container ship as a bumboat crosses the foreground. Seeing an old man pedal his trishaw past a gleaming shopping mall. }

NOWHERE IS THE counterpoint more apparent than in the Colonial District. Walk past the Palladian-style buildings, with their Doric columns, high ceilings and wide verandas skilfully adapted for the tropical climate by Singapore's Irish town surveyor, George Drumgoole Coleman. These days they stand under the shadow of buildings such as Norman Foster's ultramodern, UFO-like Supreme Court.

ORCHARD ROAD*

{ *ORCHARD ROAD: THE COMBINED CLATTER OF 10,000 PAIRS OF HEELS, THE SWISH OF DESIGNER HANDBAGS, the overwhelming, breathtaking extravagance of the boutiques, the brash mall architecture and the small pockets of sleaze still visible. There are more than 20 different malls here, each with a character all its own, and three train stations to service them. Somehow the word 'mall' isn't enough for these intimidating, monolithic consumer temples, the vast, often bizarre variety of things for sale inside them, and the world-within-a-world feeling you get every time you step into one. }

SLOUCHING TEENAGERS fill some, chattering groups of tai tais (wealthy women of leisure) eye each other in others, exchanging weary tales of maid misbehaviour. Some specialise in the singlet-and-jean uniform of the Singaporean teenage girl, while next door is a riot of Japanese streetwear, all furry boots, fluorescence, anime and meaningless English. If ever a street encapsulated the personality of a city, this is it.

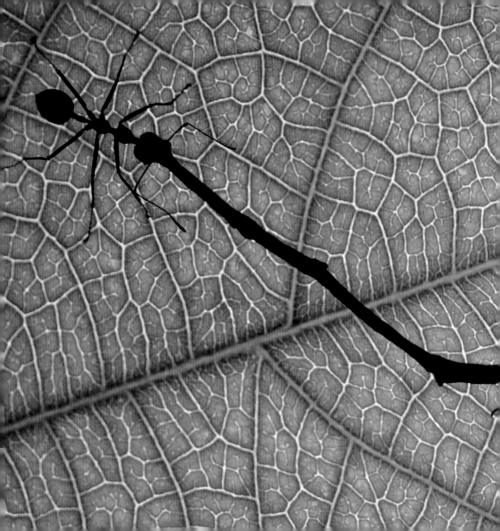

ULTRA
CLEAN*

{ *TWO MORE PIECES OF WISDOM EVERYBODY KNOWS ABOUT SINGAPORE, EVEN THOSE WHO HAVE BEEN NO FURTHER THAN THE AIRPORT.** It's spotlessly clean and completely urbanised. On the first count, they're right. Litter did not feature in Lee Kuan Yew's grand vision for his city state, nor did spitting, public urination or, famously, chewing gum. And your average Singaporean doesn't seem to find the enforced use of bins a significant inconvenience. }

IT'S NO COINCIDENCE that Singapore scores big on aesthetics, even considering its heavy reliance on high-rise concrete housing blocks, invariably surrounded by well-tended gardens, trees and shady parks. Unlike most Asian cities, the air in Singapore does not taste of exhaust fumes. The streets hum, rather than roar, with traffic. The cars here are the most expensive in the world – and while Singaporeans love to complain about their price, you suspect their lungs are not quite as unhappy about it.

BESIDES, who needs noise and pollution when the Singapore breakfast offers just that – an assault on the ears and the stomach. Sip coffee that's as strong as sump oil,

73.

{ nibble toast slathered with butter and black with charcoal from the griddle, while waiters screech orders over the din of Hokkien, Mandarin and Malay chatter. }

WHILE THE SPOTLESS streets and glistening trains surprise nobody, the number of parks and green spaces in this city often do. Some dominate their surroundings, their grand old trees competing for attention. Others nestle between buildings and surprise you as you turn a corner. Wherever you are, there's always a spot nearby where the buildings and the roads can be made to disappear, or at least dissolve into the background.

THE MIX OF architectural styles makes wandering the streets an eclectic delight, especially in Chinatown with its temples, and near the Supreme Court, which looms over the old colonial quarter like a spaceship. Many colonial buildings, such as the Old Parliament House, are being reinvented as arts venues. The spick-and-span open spaces and shopping malls often become venues for free music and dance performances ranging from zany to impenetrably avant-garde.

BEST OF ALL, these streetscapes are home to public art, like the vast chubby Bird by Colombian artist Fernando Botero in the financial district, and the People of the River sculptures that show scenes from Singapore's history along the Singapore River.

SPEAKING OF squeaky clean, the new Lasalle-SIA College of the Arts building is a remarkable, crystalline place, designed to look as if a block of ice has been dropped and shattered into six parts. The central business district also has a cluster of gleaming towers by famous Japanese architects like Kuirokawa Kisho and Tange Kenzo.

JURASSIC PARK*

{ }

* **TEN MINUTES FROM YOUR FRIENDLY LOCAL GUCCI STORE, THERE'S A FOREST THAT PRE-DATES THE ARRIVAL OF HOMO SAPIENS,** where there are more plant species than in the whole of North America. It's even believed to contain creatures as yet unknown to science.

WELCOME TO BUKIT TIMAH NATURE RESERVE, one of only two patches of primary rainforest that survive in the metropolises of the world. It's a 164-hectare nature reserve, with a range of nature walks, challenging jungle treks and six kilometres of mountain bike trails. It also has the highest point on the island, Bukit Timah (163 metres), though the dense jungle foliage doesn't let you get much of a view from its summit.

THE VISITOR CENTRE has an exhibition of the various flora and fauna that you might find in the reserve, or just wander off along some of the side trails that cut through the jungle into valleys of ferns, up to viewing points or into an old quarry.

THE WAY WE WERE*

{ ***RAMSHACKLE STILTED HOUSES WITH PEELING PAINT, THE BONES OF OLD JETTIES POKING OUT OF THE WATER,** discarded tyres and bottles flung onto the stony beach, lizards sunning themselves on the road. A short ride from Changi Beach in a chugging bumboat, the island of Pulau Ubin is the final remnant of kampong Singapore, a throwback to the 1950s and a world away from the bustling mainland (your mobile phone even welcomes you to Malaysia). Its roads wind past prawn farms, old temples and water-filled quarries, almost deserted except for cyclists. }

HERE AND THERE spooky, dilapidated abandoned houses fight a losing battle with the forest, symbols of the inevitable decline that one day soon will see Pulau Ubin's serenity sacrificed to the land pressures of the expanding mainland population. Public protests have won a rare victory against the government, granting a reprieve to the ecologically valuable Chek Jawa mangroves when they were threatened with development, but it's only probably a matter of time.

A FINE CITY*

* THE ARCANE SUBJECT OF CIVIC LAW HAS NEVER MADE A CITY SO FAMOUS.
At one time travellers could even be denied entry to Singapore for having long hair or being dressed like a hippy. And ever since the wrath of the US media was invoked by Singapore's decision to cane a teenage American who vandalised several cars, the city's strict system of fines has been a source of amusement for the world and the inspiration for thousands of tacky T-shirts. Yes, Singapore is a Fine City. It's $1,000 for littering. $500 for smoking in a public place. $50 for jaywalking. $0 for selling subversive T-shirts. Commit to memory and recite next time you step in a dog turd at home.

THE CITY'S NOTORIOUSLY heavy penalties for relatively minor offences usually attract derisive sniggers in the West, as if fast-food wrappers and plastic bottles in gutters were an integral part of a city, but this place certainly manages without them.

MASS TRANSIT*

{ *** ROADS LIKE PIECES OF LANDSCAPE ART, OVERHUNG WITH GIANT RAIN TREES AND EDGED WITH FLOWERS, TRAINS GLEAMING LIKE DINNER PLATES,** graffiti-free bus seats... even the pedestrian bridges look like garden centres. In Singapore, mass transport is an exercise in urban aesthetics in which concrete and tarmac are simply not permitted to look ugly. }

THE MRT NORTH EAST LINE, which opened in 2003, has some interesting murals. Husband and wife team Milenko and Delia Prvacki illuminated Dhoby Ghaut Station with intricate swirling murals; Outram Park has bas-reliefs of local scenes by Teo Eng Seng that look like people set in plaster while playing soccer or shopping.

HAVING INVESTED squillions into its public transport infrastructure, Singapore is without doubt the easiest city in Asia to get around. You rarely have to wait more than a few minutes for a bus and they will take you almost anywhere you want to go. Some even have TVs.

PARKLIFE*

{ }

* OLD MEN PEDAL RUSTY BIKES TO THE POND, FISHING ROD AND BUCKET DANGLING FROM A HANDLEBAR, dog peering eagerly from the shopping basket. Under the mouldering wall of a 19th-century Chinatown mosque, an office worker sleeps during his lunch hour.

ROLLERBLADERS RACE along the seaside East Coast Park, rock climbers scale the crumbling face of a Bukit Timah cliff, kayakers unsettle the terrapins in MacRitchie, birdwatchers crouch in the hides of Sungei Buloh and skateboarders practise kickflips behind the Orchard Road malls.

THERE ARE MORE than 100 city parks, and like little green fingerprints, each has its own unique character. They're shaped and manicured, imaginatively designed and filled with facilities like bike tracks, fitness trails, playgrounds, fish ponds and cafés. Many are linked by Park Connectors, bike trails that thread through the city and allow runners and cyclists to travel long distances untroubled by cars.

84.

A GREEN HEART *

{ *** SINGAPORE IS AN URBAN DOUGHNUT, BUT THE HOLE IS FILLED WITH THICK FORESTS AND RESERVOIRS.** The green centre of the island is a wonderland of peace, where the occasional buzz of a plane overhead is the only indication that a city of 4.5 million people surrounds you. Here your only neighbours are raucous birds and families of macaque monkeys that eye you calmly and unnervingly as you tiptoe past. }

THE FOUR HUGE reservoirs don't just serve the utilitarian purpose of providing a thirsty metropolis with water. They're like visual sedatives, the only vessel-free expanses of water around the city – you can allow yourself the illusion that you're by a vast jungle lake, until the family of eight plonks their picnic in front of you.

AROUND THE EDGES of the green heart are golf courses and country clubs, and the world-class Singapore Zoological Gardens, which house 3600 animals including the endangered white rhino and white Bengal tigers.

YOU CAN'T BEAT the magnificent Botanic Gardens, established around 1860 when they were used as a test ground for crops such as rubber. There's a four-hectare patch of the original Singaporean jungle that once covered the entire island, an extraordinary orchid garden displaying over 60,000 orchids, a library with material dating from the 16th century, a dignified lake with a shell-like stage built in the centre, and more than 600,000 botanical specimens. Visit the gardens just after dawn, as the sun burns the mist off the rolling lawns.

90.

GOLD STAR

SINGAPORE, GO TO THE TOP
OF THE CLASS FOR FOOD.
NOWHERE ELSE IN ASIA CAN
YOU FIND SUCH A VARIETY OF
INCREDIBLE EDIBLES, IN SUCH
QUANTITY AND SO EASILY
ACCESSIBLE – JUST ORDER,
SIT AND STUFF.

MY PERFECT DAY

MAT OAKLEY

{ * Start early, amid the chatter of an old kopitiam (breakfast and coffee shop), for hot sweet kopi, runny eggs and kaya toast, slapped onto your table without ceremony. Once you're loaded with cholesterol, take a stroll in the magnificent Botanic Gardens, then along Orchard Road before the crowds hit. Head down into the MRT, up one stop to Little India and out into another world of grubby streets and food markets, and dip your hands into a curry lunch – fiery fuel for a walk to the mosques, carpet sellers and coffee houses of Kampong Glam, the Muslim Quarter. After a cardamom coffee or hot mint tea, take a bus to Chinatown and browse through the antique shops, street markets and teashops. A few steamed dumplings and tea from a Chinatown café, then leave the city for the green centre, and Singapore's zoo and peerless Night Safari. After seeing the sunset with the leopards, do a taxi race down the flawless, tree-lined expressway to Newton Circus, the city's most famous hawker centre. Bursting with seafood and beer, take another taxi to Raffles Hotel for a cocktail. Energy permitting, dance your way into the early hours with the beautiful people at Zouk, Singapore's thumping megaclub.

SON OF A SCOUSE GIT AND AN ASPIC JELLY-EATING YORKSHIRE WOMAN, MAT WAS BORN IN THE ENGLISH TOWN OF WATFORD, WHOSE RESIDENTS ARE FAMOUS FOR NOT WANTING TO LIVE IN WATFORD ANYMORE. He has spent the last 18 months living in Singapore with his girlfriend and a couple of badly behaved Fijian cats. Besides paddling and walking at the MacRitchie Reservoir, pedalling on Pulau Ubin, eating sambal stingray at Newton Circus and drinking mojitos at the Post Bar, his most memorable Singapore experience was standing in the Penny Black with a local branch of the Liverpool Supporters' Club, watching the 2005 European Cup Final.

PHOTO CREDITS

}

CITIESCAPE

SINGAPORE

OCTOBER 2006

**PUBLISHED BY LONELY PLANET
PUBLICATIONS PTY LTD**
ABN 36 005 607 983
90 Maribyrnong St, Footscray,
Victoria 3011, Australia
www.lonelyplanet.com

Printed through Colorcraft Ltd, Hong Kong.
Printed in China.

PHOTOGRAPHS
Many of the images in this book are available
for licensing from Lonely Planet Images.
www.lonelyplanetimages.com

ISBN 1 74104 940 7

© Lonely Planet 2006
© photographers as indicated 2006

LONELY PLANET OFFICES
AUSTRALIA Locked Bag 1, Footscray, Victoria 3011
Telephone 03 8379 8000 Fax 03 8379 8111
Email talk2us@lonelyplanet.com.au

USA 150 Linden St, Oakland, CA 94607
Telephone 510 893 8555 TOLL FREE 800 275 8555
Fax 510 893 8572 Email info@lonelyplanet.com

UK 72–82 Rosebery Ave, London EC1R 4RW
Telephone 020 7841 9000 Fax 020 7841 9001
Email go@lonelyplanet.co.uk

Publisher ROZ HOPKINS
Commissioning Editor ELLIE COBB
Editors JOCELYN HAREWOOD, VANESSA BATTERSBY
Design MARK ADAMS
Layout Designer INDRA KILFOYLE
Image Researcher PEPI BLUCK
Pre-press Production GERARD WALKER
Project Managers ANNELIES MERTENS, ADAM MCCROW
Publishing Planning Manager JO VRACA
Print Production Manager GRAHAM IMESON